SUN, HEAT AND THE ENERGY FOR LIFE

Renewable and Non-Renewable Source of Energy

Self Taught Physics | Science Grade 3 | Children's Physics Books

BABY PROFESSOR
EDUCATION KIDS

First Edition, 2021

Published in the United States by Speedy Publishing LLC, 40 E Main Street, Newark, Delaware 19711 USA.

© 2021 Baby Professor Books, an imprint of Speedy Publishing LLC

All rights reserved.

Without limiting the rights under the copyright reserved above, no part of this publication may be reproduced, stored in or introduced into a retrieval system, or transmitted, in any form, or by any means (electronic, mechanical, photocopying, recording, or otherwise), without the prior written permission of the copyright owner.

All images in this book have been reproduced with the knowledge and prior consent of the artists concerned, and no responsibility is accepted by producer, publisher, or printer for any infringement of copyright or otherwise arising from the contents of this publication.

Baby Professor Books are available at special discounts when purchased in bulk for industrial and sales-promotional use. For details contact our Special Sales Team at Speedy Publishing LLC, 40 E Main Street, Newark, Delaware 19711 USA. Telephone (888) 248-4521 Fax: (210) 519-4043.

10 9 8 7 6 * 5 4 3 2 1

Print Edition: 9781541949188
Digital Edition: 9781541950986
Hardcover Edition: 9781541975712

See the world in pictures. Build your knowledge in style.
www.speedypublishing.com

Table of Contents

Chapter One:
Energy from the Sun 9

Chapter Two:
Food Energy 25

Chapter Three:
Renewable and Non-renewable Sources of Energy 53

Have you ever felt worn out after exercising? Have you ever felt exhausted from staying up too late? All living creatures require energy to sustain themselves. When their energy supplies run low, they need to be replenished.

When all living creatures' energy supplies run low, they need to be replenished.

The Sun is the major source of energy for the entire planet Earth.

There are several different sources of energy that are important to sustain life on Earth. Some sources of energy can be used over and over while others will eventually be used up entirely. This book will look at the Sun, the major source of energy for the entire planet Earth, as well as other forms of energy. The book will focus on these different types of energy sources and explain them. It will also speak about the importance of being mindful of taking care of energy sources.

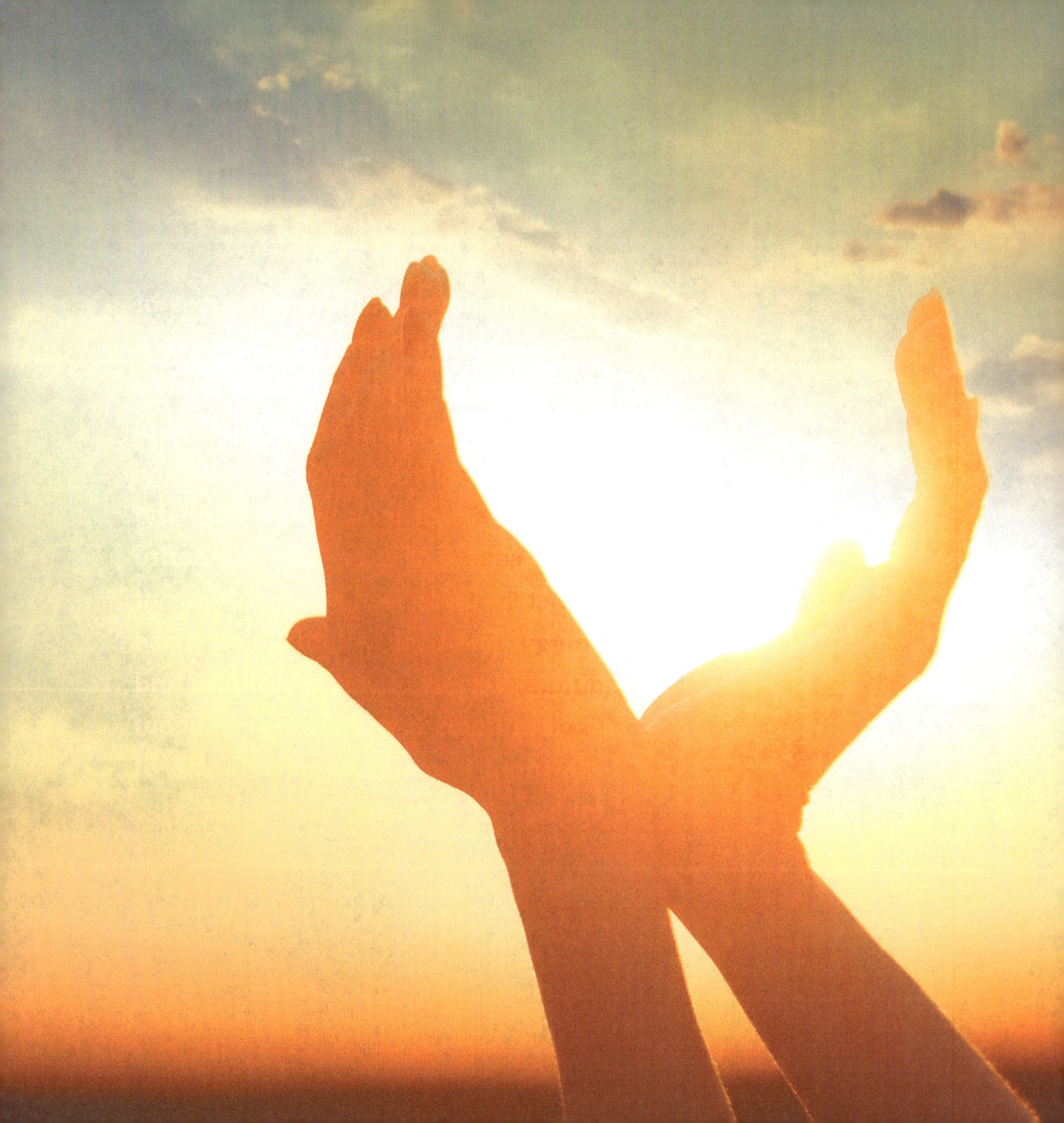

Chapter One

Energy from the Sun

The Sun is the number one source of energy on Earth and without it, life as we know it would not be possible.

The sun

When sunlight comes to the Earth, we recognize it as light energy.

Light and Heat Energy from the Sun:

Energy that comes from the Sun is called solar energy. We can detect it in sunlight. When sunlight comes to the Earth, we recognize it as light energy. It illuminates the Earth so that we can see during the daytime. It also works as a source of energy for plants to make food. These plants, in turn, feed animals.

When the sunlight hits an object, it is transformed into heat or thermal energy. This energy is also critical to life. Living organisms have adapted to life at specific temperatures. Some animals do better in hotter regions while others in colder areas. However, the Sun ensures that the temperature is never so cold that life cannot survive at some area on the Earth.

The Sun ensures that the temperature is never so cold that life cannot survive at some area on the Earth.

A green lizard lying on a stone, basking in the sun.

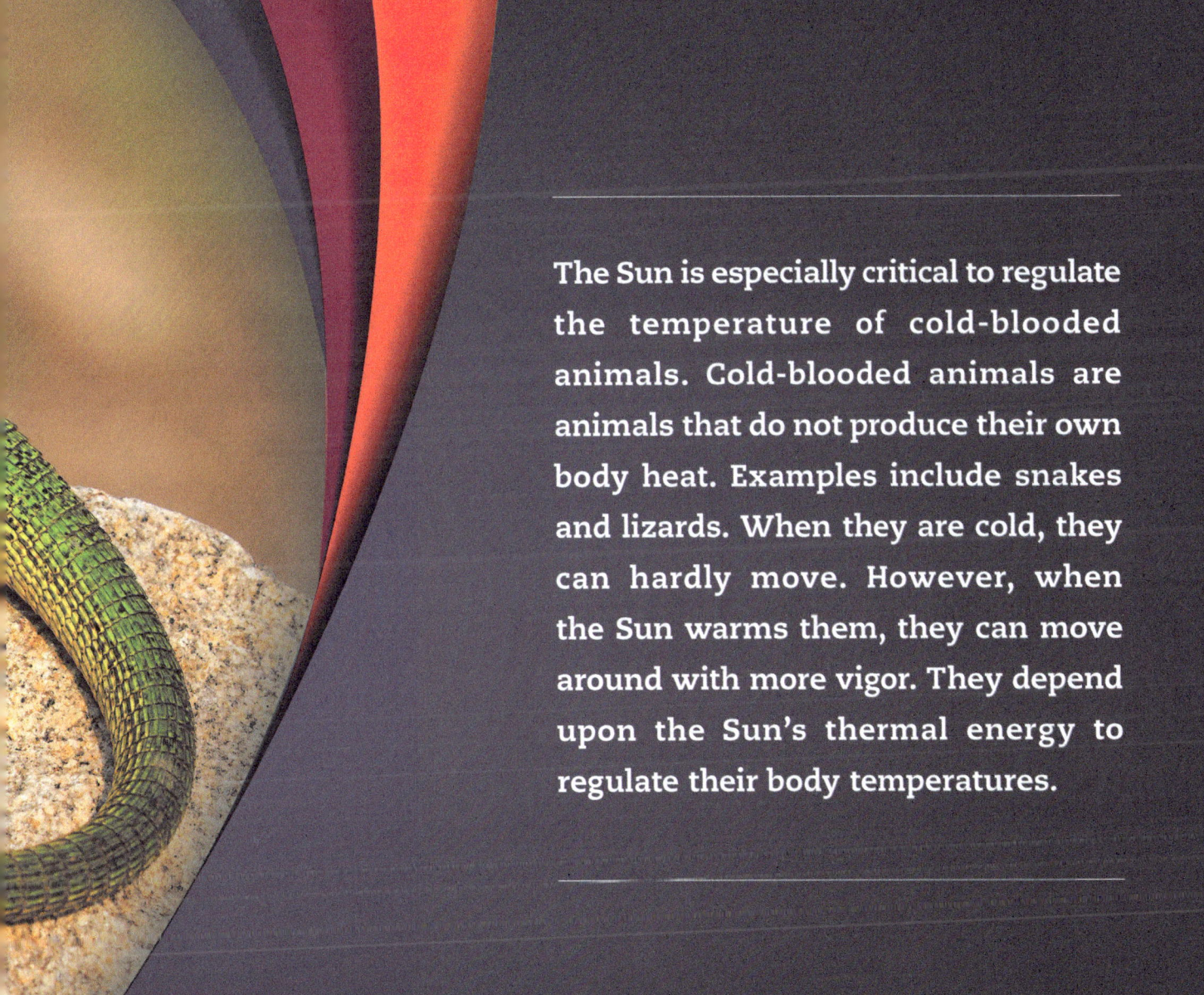

The Sun is especially critical to regulate the temperature of cold-blooded animals. Cold-blooded animals are animals that do not produce their own body heat. Examples include snakes and lizards. When they are cold, they can hardly move. However, when the Sun warms them, they can move around with more vigor. They depend upon the Sun's thermal energy to regulate their body temperatures.

Photosynthesis:

Photosynthesis is the name given to the process where plants use sunlight as an energy source to produce their own food. Photosynthesis is essential to life on Earth. Animals eat plants and other animals to survive since they cannot make their own food. If plants could not harness energy from the Sun to provide food for themselves, and in turn to the animals that eat them, all life on Earth would likely cease to exist.

Photosynthesis is the process where plants use sunlight as an energy source to produce their own food.

PLANT PHOTOSYNTHESIS

Sunlight

Carbon dioxide

Oxygen

Sugar

Minerals

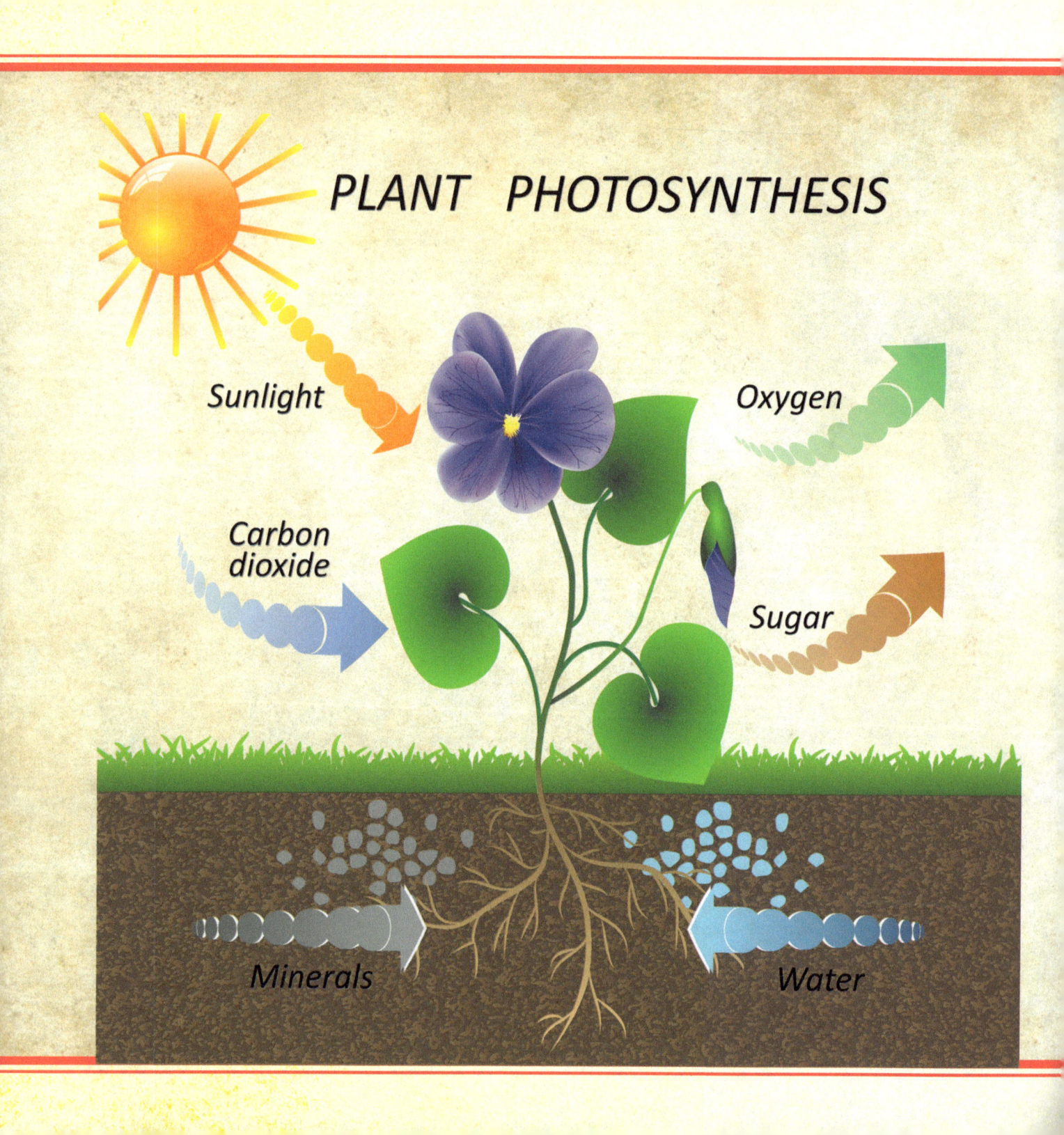

Water

Photosynthesis captures sunlight through chlorophyll which is what makes plants green. The energy provided by the Sun helps to break down water and carbon dioxide gas that the plants absorb through their roots and leaves. From the raw material broken down, plants create sugar and oxygen. Oxygen is a waste product, and it is released into the air, but sugar is a food source for the plant. The sugar that the plant does not immediately use can be stored away for later.

The oxygen which is produced by plants is equally important since most animals require oxygen to breathe. The waste gas that animals produce is carbon dioxide gas. As a result, there is a cyclical relationship. Plants keep our air quality good by giving off oxygen, and we provide carbon dioxide for them.

OXYGEN CYCLE

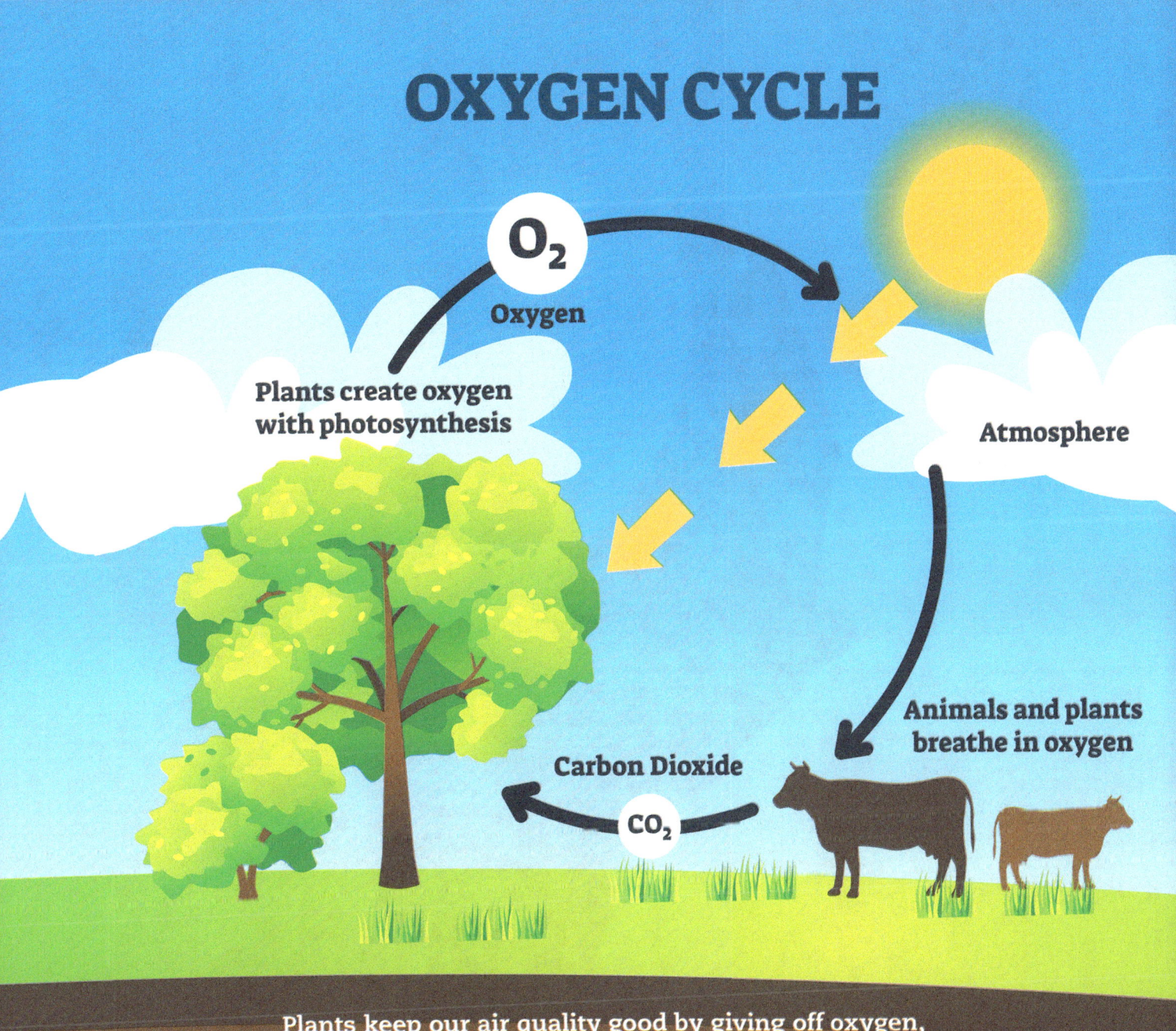

O₂ Oxygen

Plants create oxygen with photosynthesis

Atmosphere

Animals and plants breathe in oxygen

Carbon Dioxide CO₂

Plants keep our air quality good by giving off oxygen, and we provide carbon dioxide for them.

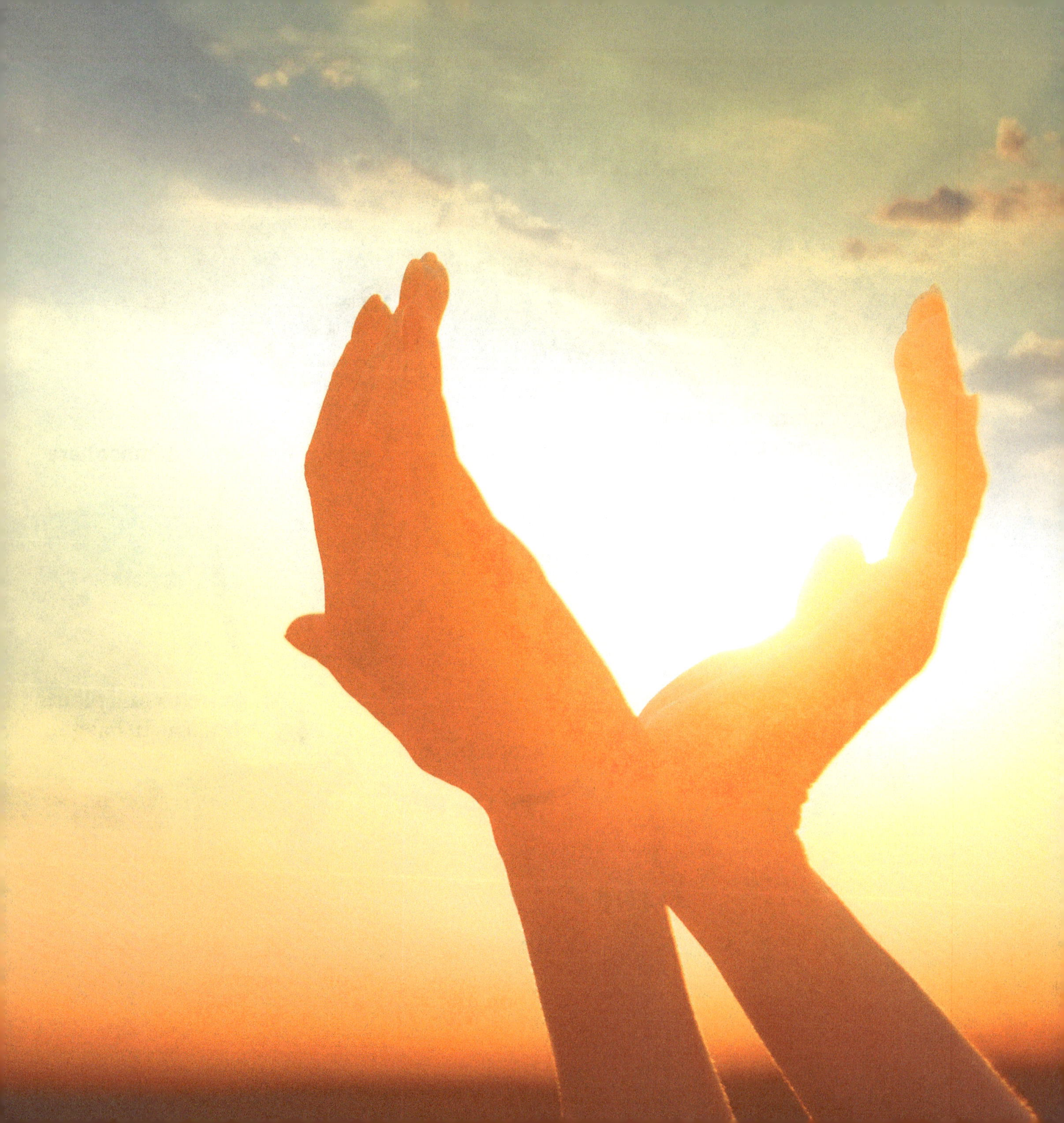

Chapter Two
Food Energy

We spoke about how animals need food and how plants make their own food. However, how does food provide energy? This chapter will offer the explanation so read on to learn about food and chemical energy.

Giraffes eating the leaves of a trees.

97 kcal
42 kcal
32 kcal
21 kcal
57 kcal
33 kcal
40 kcal
52 kcal
CALORIES
60 kcal
50 kcal
75 kcal
15 kcal

Fruits and vegetables with calories labels

Calories:

Calories are how we measure how much energy food contains. It is the amount of energy required to raise one gram of water by one degree Celsius. It used to be measured in something called a calorimeter where the food would be burned. However, now it can be calculated mathematically by looking at what is in the food and counting the known calories.

The energy in food is chemical energy. Chemical energy is energy that is found in the bonds that hold atoms and molecules together. Atoms are the smallest whole part of matter. Matter makes up everything in the Universe. Molecules are made up of two or more atoms bound together.

The structure of matter

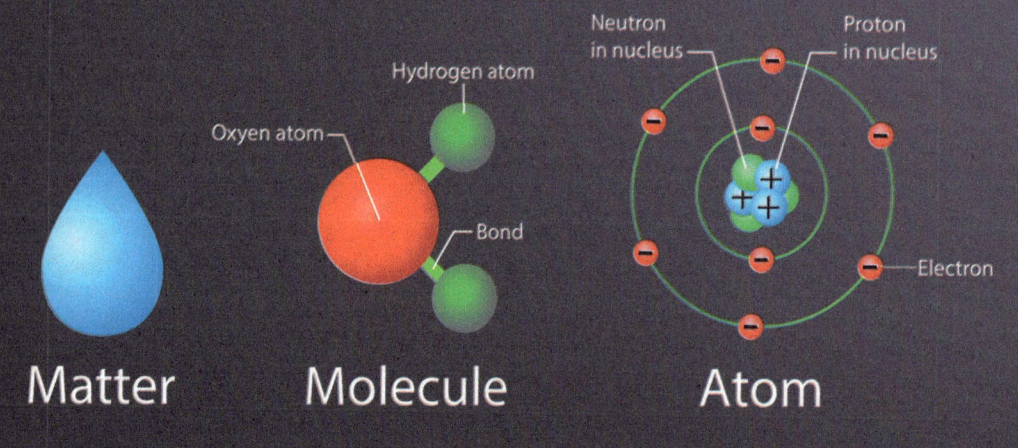

Hydrogen atom
Oxyen atom
Bond
Neutron in nucleus
Proton in nucleus
Electron

Matter   Molecule   Atom

The energy in food is chemical energy.

When food is digested, it is broken down so that the chemical energy can be released.

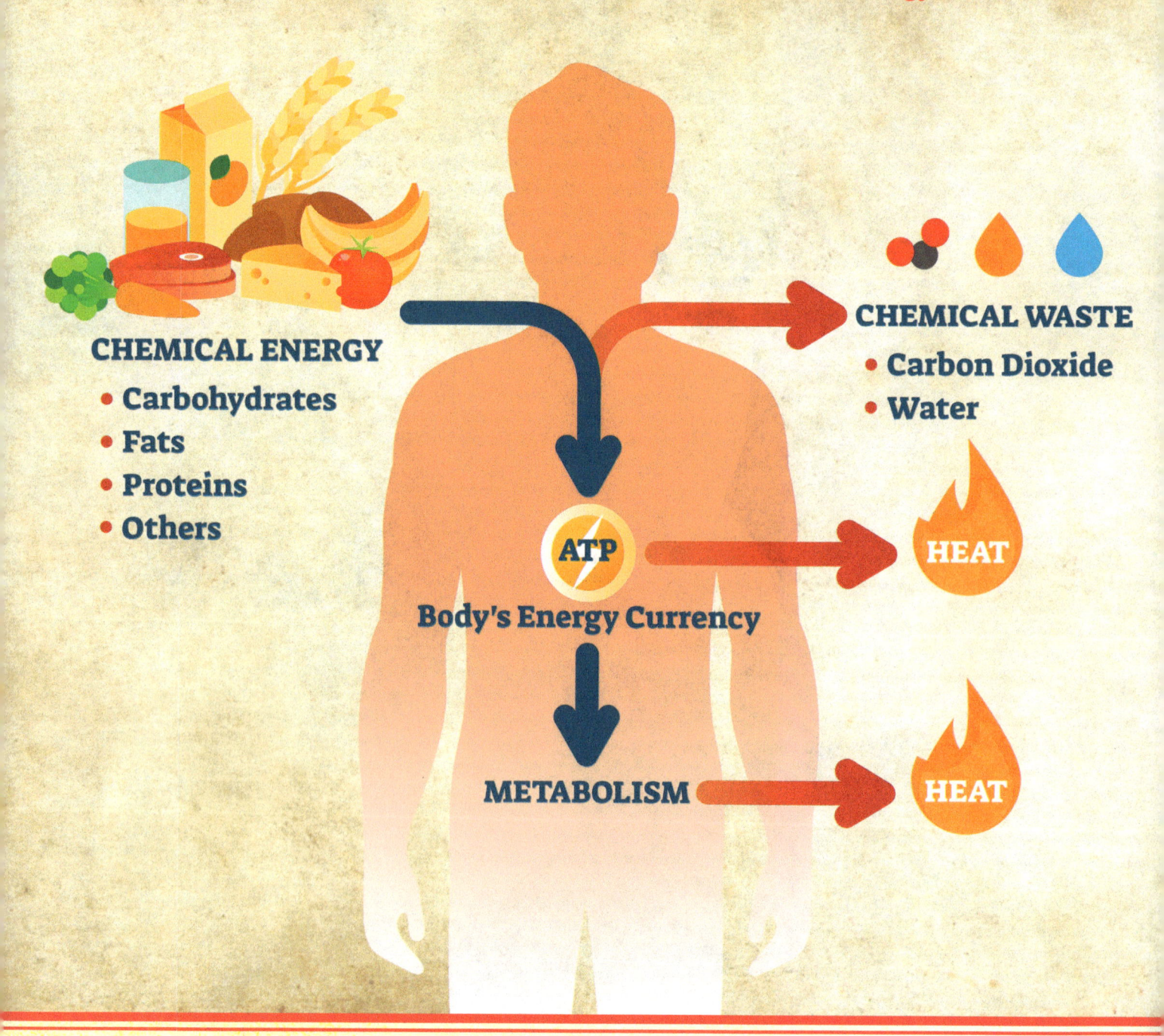

CHEMICAL ENERGY
- Carbohydrates
- Fats
- Proteins
- Others

ATP
Body's Energy Currency

METABOLISM

CHEMICAL WASTE
- Carbon Dioxide
- Water

HEAT

HEAT

When you digest food, the food is broken down so that the chemical energy can be released. This energy is then used for everything that the body does, from repairing damaged cells to even sleeping. What is not used by the body immediately is stored as fat.

How much food someone needs to eat depends on many factors from their age, their sex, to their job. Men generally need more than women. Athletes need more than non-athletes.

Men generally need more food than women.

When people are trying to lose weight, they will often decrease their caloric intake.

When people are trying to lose weight, they will often decrease their caloric intake so that their body will burn off fat for energy. Exercise can also be important in maintaining a healthy weight.

Carbohydrates:

Carbohydrates are the main source of energy in food. Food can provide us with minerals, vitamins, and other nutrition that the body needs to repair itself. However, the energy source is found in carbohydrates. Carbohydrates can be found in starchy foods like peas or potatoes and grains like bread or pasta. Starch is a complex sugar that can be used by plants to store their excess sugar. Unlike glucose or sucrose, types of sugar, starch does not taste sweet.

Carbohydrates can be found in starchy foods like peas or potatoes and grains like bread or pasta.

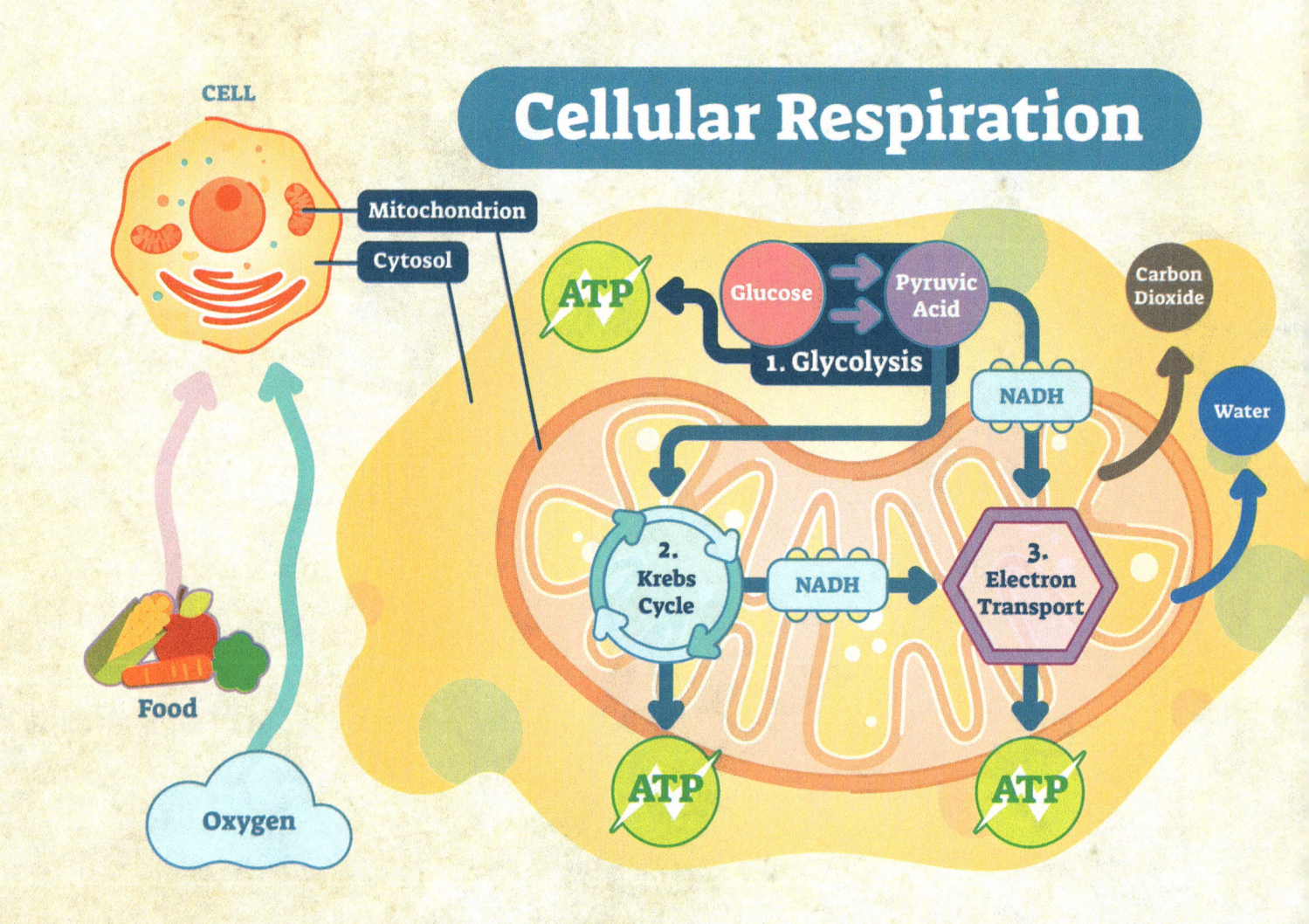

Cellular Respiration

CELL
- Mitochondrion
- Cytosol

Food

Oxygen

1. Glycolysis: Glucose → Pyruvic Acid → ATP

NADH

2. Krebs Cycle → ATP

NADH →

3. Electron Transport → ATP

Carbon Dioxide

Water

All carbohydrates that are digested will be converted into glucose sugar. The digestive tract includes everything from your mouth to your stomach and intestines. This sugar then enters our bloodstream. It is glucose which is broken down in a process called cellular respiration to provide the body with energy.

Iodine is used by scientists to test for the presence of starch. When iodine is placed on starch, it turns from a muddy yellow color into a deep blue or purple color. You can test this reaction for yourself.

Iodine test for Starch

Detect starch or complex carbohydrate in organic sample

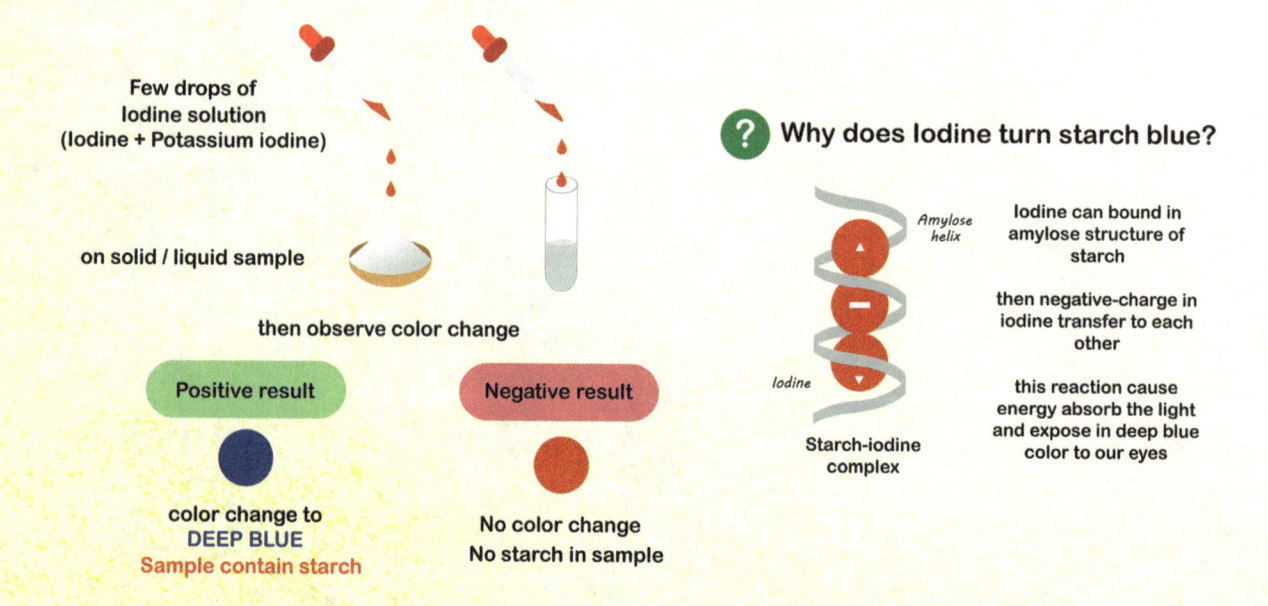

Few drops of
Iodine solution
(Iodine + Potassium iodine)

on solid / liquid sample

then observe color change

Positive result

color change to
DEEP BLUE
Sample contain starch

Negative result

No color change
No starch in sample

? Why does Iodine turn starch blue?

Amylose helix

Iodine

Starch-iodine complex

Iodine can bound in amylose structure of starch

then negative-charge in iodine transfer to each other

this reaction cause energy absorb the light and expose in deep blue color to our eyes

A bottle of iodine

Get a paper plate, a bottle of iodine, and a medicine dropper. Also, cut up some carrots, potato, apple, banana, and celery. Place each piece on the plate and drop some iodine on top. Which ones caused the iodine to change color? Record your results.

The food pieces that change into a deep blue contained starch. The other contained sugars. Potato and celery contain starch.

Potatoes

Celery

Apple, bananas, and carrots

Apples, bananas, and carrots have some starch, but they mostly have sugars. For this reason, they taste sweeter.

The Food Chain:

The ultimate source of all these carbohydrates comes from producers. Producers are what we call organisms that can make their own food and do not have to rely on eating something else to gain sugar for energy. Generally, plants are the producers, and they are at the bottom of the food chain.

Plants are the producers, and they are at the bottom of the food chain.

Any organisms that eat the producers or eat another consumer, or both, are called consumers. Herbivores are those organisms that eat only plants. Carnivores eat only meat. Omnivores eat both.

carnivores

omnivores

herbivores

Illustration of herbivores, omnivores, and carnivores.

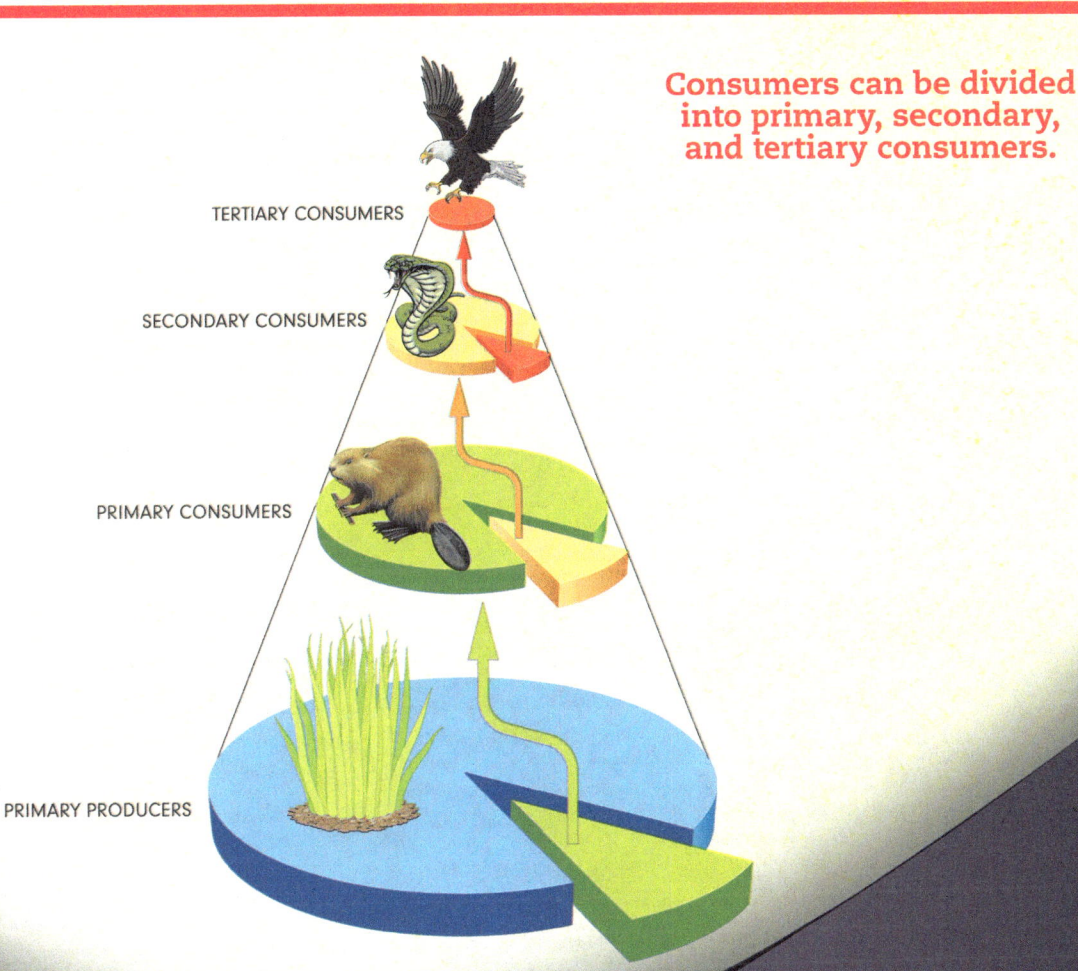

Consumers can be divided into primary, secondary, and tertiary consumers.

TERTIARY CONSUMERS

SECONDARY CONSUMERS

PRIMARY CONSUMERS

PRIMARY PRODUCERS

Consumers can be divided into primary, secondary, and tertiary consumers. Primary consumers are the first consumers, and they eat plants. Secondary consumers eat the primary consumers and tertiary consumers would eat the secondary consumers.

Shelf fungus decomposing a fallen tree.

There are also decomposers. Decomposers break down animals that are already dead. In doing so, they return the nutrients that were left in dead bodies of animals or plants, back to the Earth. In this way, plants can re-absorb the nutrients to be healthy, and this creates a cycle that sustains the food chain.

There is a reason that most food chains do not have more than four or five tiers called trophic levels. This is because the process of energy transference through eating is imperfect. A great deal of energy is lost. Those organisms that are on the top of a food chain must eat more to sustain themselves. Most of the energy is contained in the producers. Plants also have the greatest combined biomass.

FOOD CHAIN

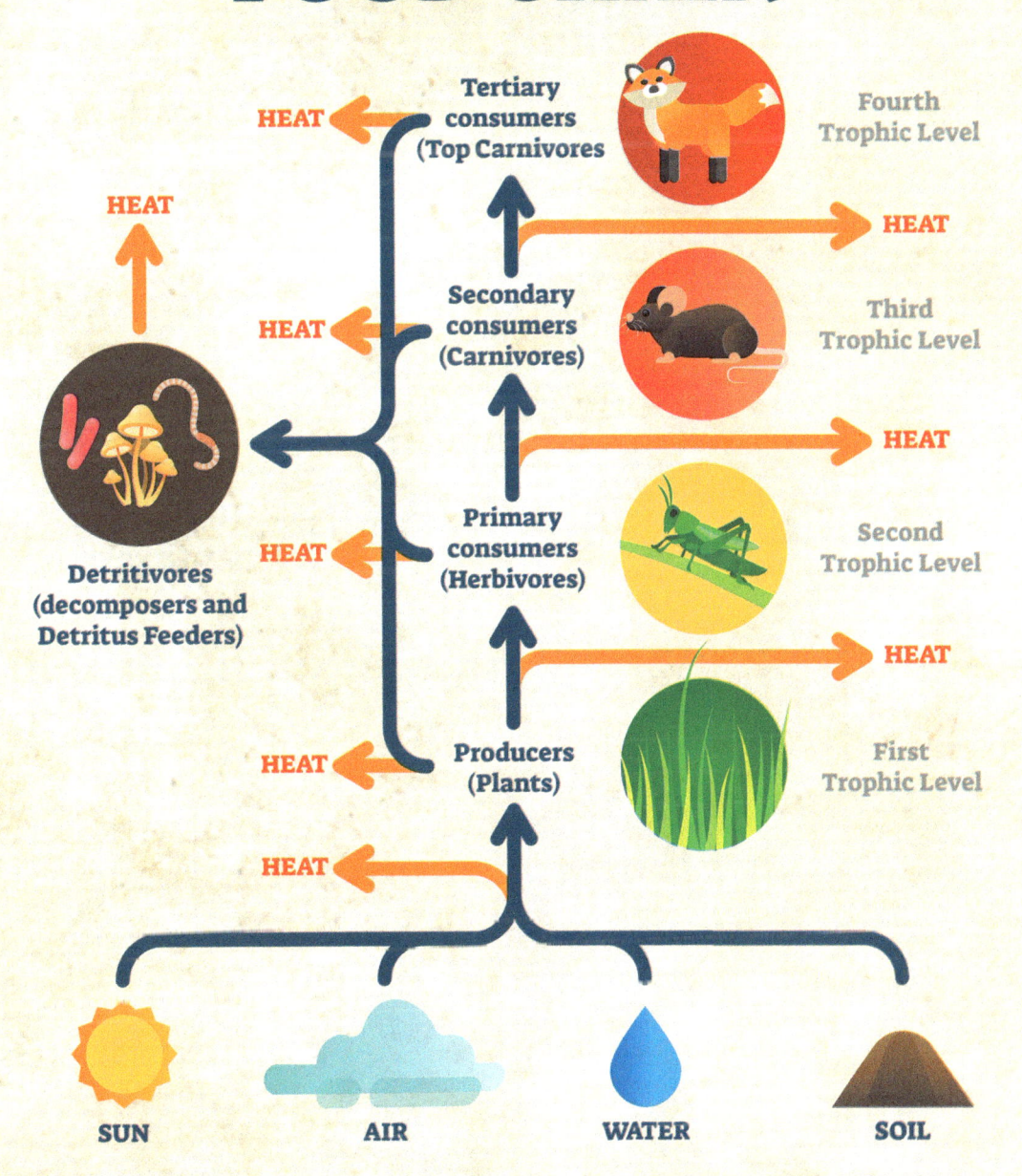

Tertiary consumers (Top Carnivores) — Fourth Trophic Level

Secondary consumers (Carnivores) — Third Trophic Level

Primary consumers (Herbivores) — Second Trophic Level

Producers (Plants) — First Trophic Level

Detritivores (decomposers and Detritus Feeders)

SUN AIR WATER SOIL

Most food chains do not have more than four or five tiers called trophic levels.

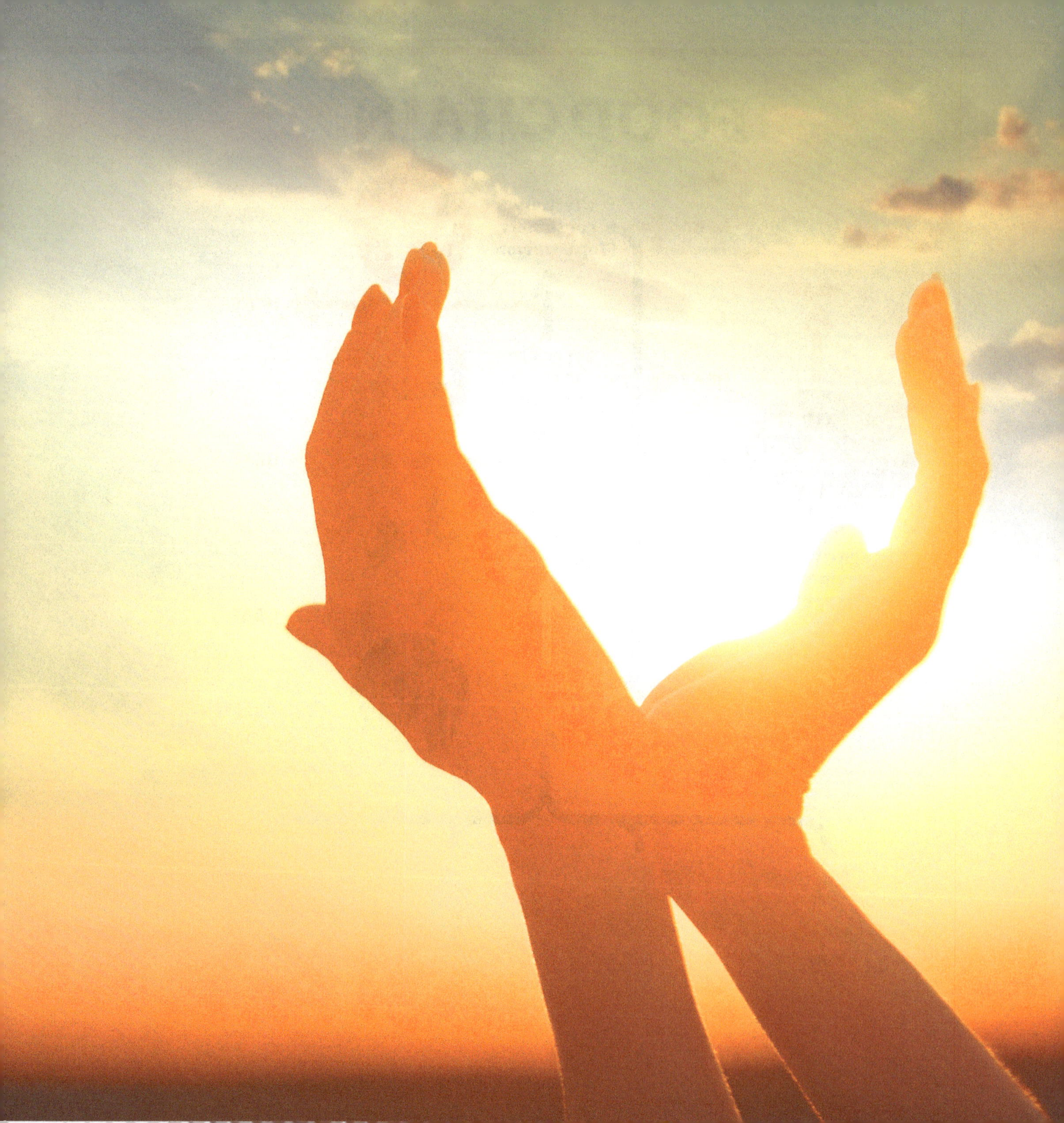

/ CHAPTER THREE

Renewable and Non-Renewable Sources of Energy

Humans live with the expectation of not only requiring energy to sustain their bodies, but also to enhance their lives. In our everyday lives, we have heating, the Internet, television, cellphones, and many more things besides. All these items require energy as well. The sources which provide power or energy to these items can either be renewable or non-renewable energy sources.

The sources which provide power or energy to these items can either be renewable or non-renewable energy sources.

Renewable Energy

WIND ENERGY — Conversion of wind kinetic energy into electrical

HYDROPOWER ENERGY — Converting energy of water flow into electrical energy

BIOMASS ENERGY — Plant materials can be transformed into energy

GEOTHERMAL ENERGY — The energy contained in the ground

SOLAR ENERGY — The use of solar radiation for energy

A renewable energy source is one that can be used without worrying that it will run out.

Renewable Energy Sources:

A renewable energy source is one that can be used without worrying that it will run out. However, while renewable sources cannot be easily used up, they can be polluted. Examples of renewable energy sources are solar, wind, water, and geothermal energy.

Solar energy produces enough energy to run all our needs for an entire year in forty minutes! However, it is difficult and expensive to capture. Currently, technology called photovoltaic or PV cells have been used to capture the Sun's energy to generate electricity. It is also used for heat. This is called solar heating.

PV cells have been used to capture the Sun's energy to generate electricity.

A wind farm in Hesse, Germany.

Wind and water energy work by using turbines. As these turbines spin, they convert the energy into electrical energy using something called a generator. The movement of the water can cause the turbines to spin, or the blowing of the wind can. When there are multiple wind turbines in an area, it is called a wind farm.

Geothermal energy comes from the heat that is built up inside the Earth. In places like Iceland, for example, the heat is close enough to the surface, that it can be easily reached for energy. In other parts of the world, much drilling would be required.

Geothermal power plant located at Reykjanes peninsula in Iceland.

OIL AND GAS NATURAL FORMATION

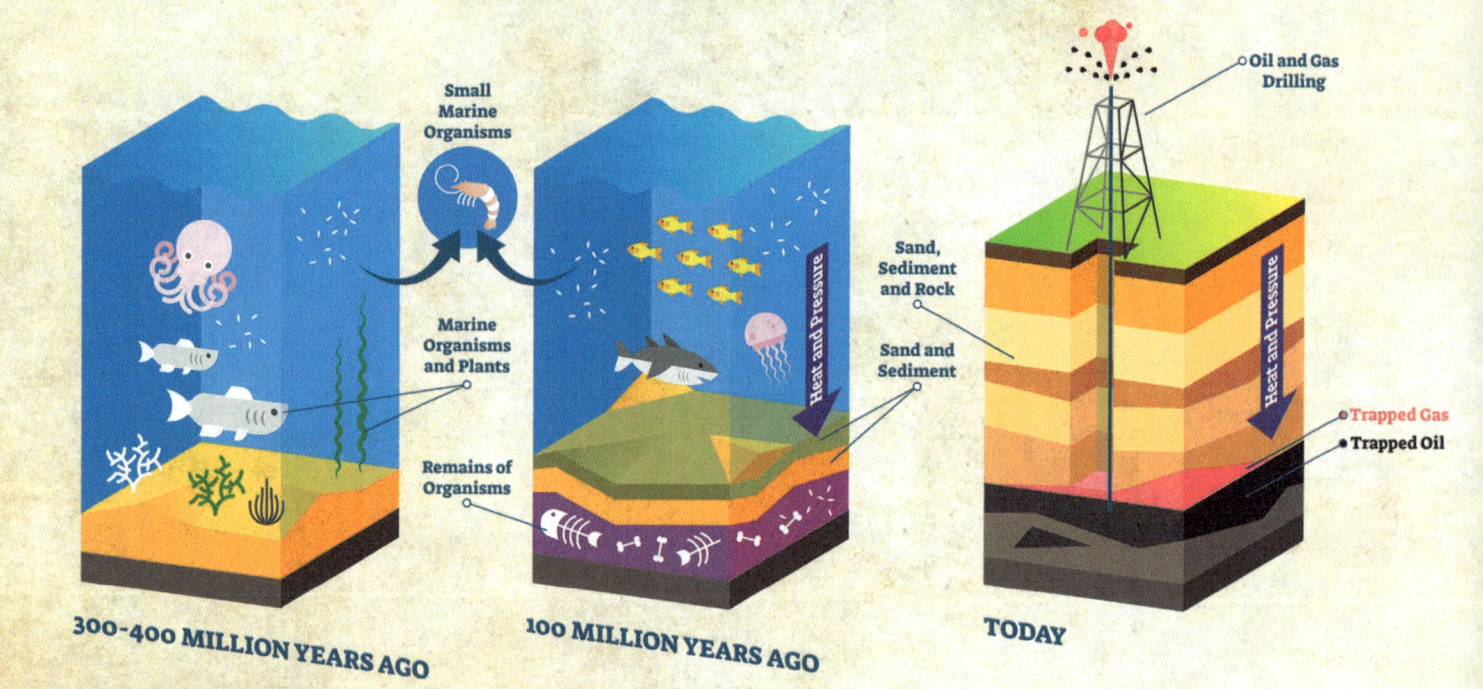

300-400 MILLION YEARS AGO

- Small Marine Organisms
- Marine Organisms and Plants
- Remains of Organisms

100 MILLION YEARS AGO

- Sand, Sediment and Rock
- Sand and Sediment
- Heat and Pressure

TODAY

- Oil and Gas Drilling
- Heat and Pressure
- Trapped Gas
- Trapped Oil

Marine Organisms → *Time and Pressure* → Remains of Organisms → *Time and Pressure* → Natural Oil and Gass

Non-renewable Energy Sources:

Unfortunately, much of our energy is derived from non-renewable sources. Fossil fuels like coal, oil, and petroleum are all quite common. Fossil fuels are created over thousands to millions of years. They are formed from the remains of animals and plants that are compressed underground at extreme pressures. They are non-renewable because they can take such a long time to form. We will use fossil fuels up before more can be made!

Another downside of these energy sources is that they can generate a lot of pollution. The burning of fossil fuels, for example, emits a great deal of fumes into the air. This can cause air pollution which can be harmful.

Coal burning power plant with smoke stacks, Moscow, Russia.

Offshore oil rig drilling platform in the gulf of Thailand.

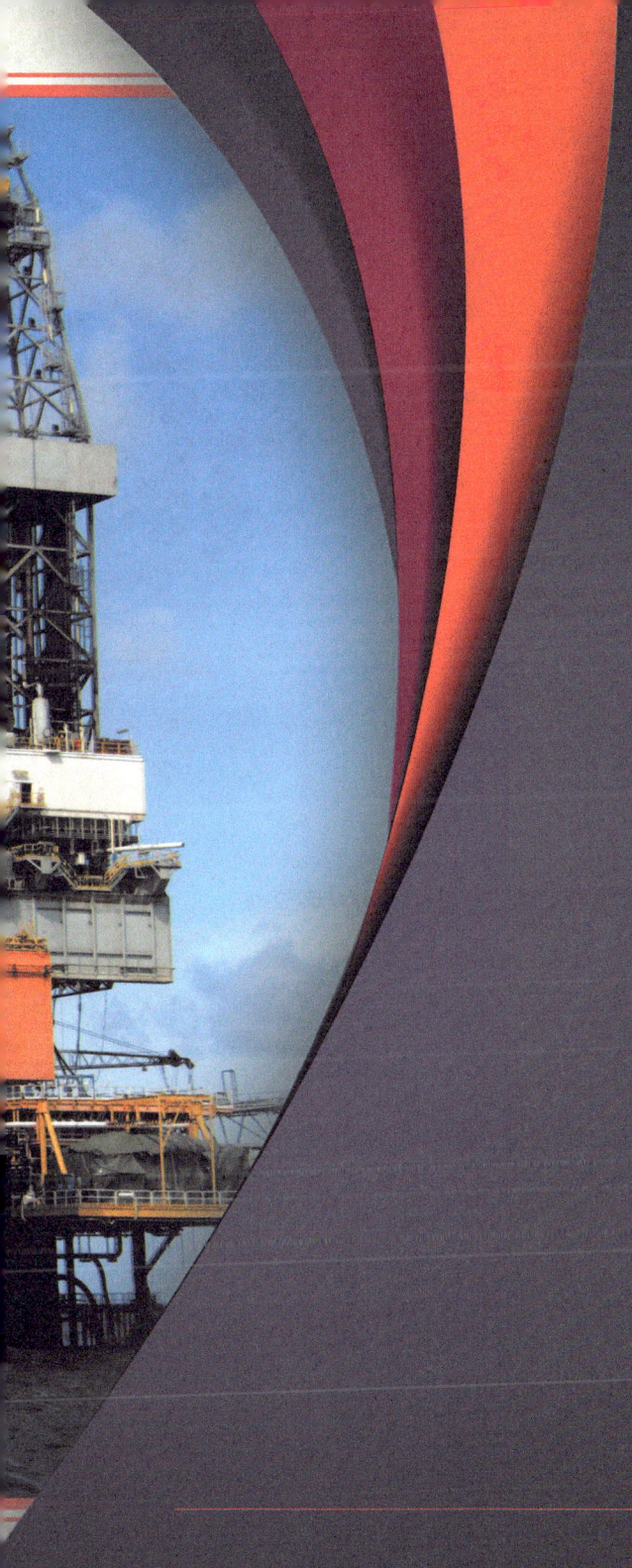

Finally, the drilling and mining for fossil fuels can be hazardous and bad on the environment. Laws have been made and are being made to try and reduce the amount of damage done. Nevertheless, there is increasing pressure to try and transition to cleaner and renewable sources of energy. It is hoped that in time the transition can be made.

There are many different types of energy. Organisms rely on energy to sustain their lives. In addition, people have harnessed energy from different sources to improve the quality of our lives. Nonetheless, some energy sources are in danger of being used up, and some have resulted in pollution to the environment.

Visit

www.speedypublishing.com

To view and download free content on your favorite subject and browse our catalog of new and exciting books for readers of all ages.

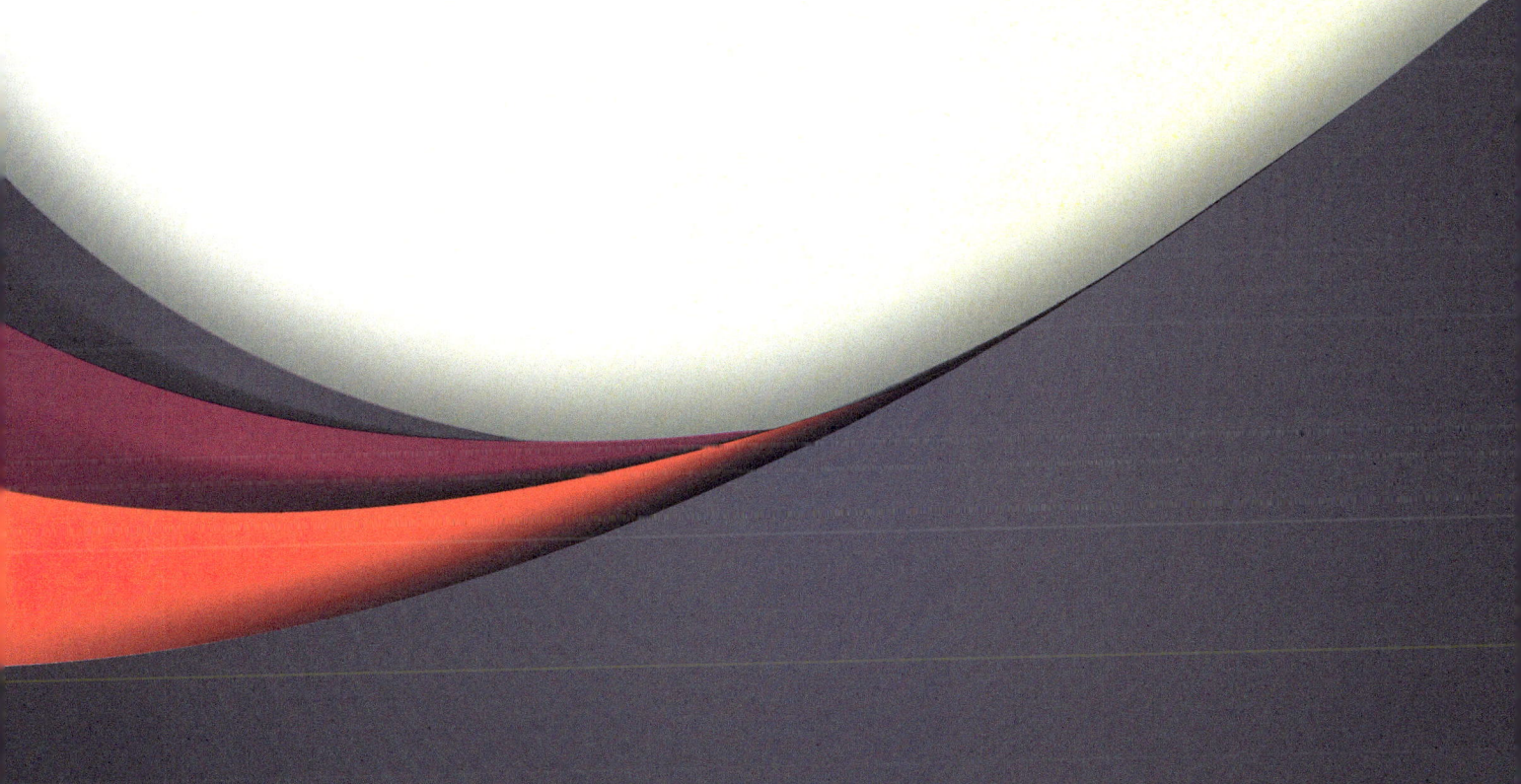

Made in the USA
Columbia, SC
15 May 2025